HOW TO GUIDE
GIRL SCOUT JUNIORS ON

AGENT
OF CHANGE

IT'S YOUR WORLD—CHANGE IT! A LEADERSHIP JOURNEY

Girl Scouts of the USA

CHAIR, NATIONAL BOARD OF DIRECTORS	CHIEF EXECUTIVE OFFICER	EXECUTIVE VICE PRESIDENT, MISSION TO MARKET	VICE PRESIDENT, PROGRAM DEVELOPMENT
Patricia Diaz Dennis	Kathy Cloninger	Norma I. Barquet	Eileen Doyle

JUNIOR WRITING CIRCLE: Jana Martin, Ann Redpath, Laura Tuchman

CONTRIBUTORS: Kate Gottlieb, Toi James, Maja Ninkovic

ILLUSTRATED BY Christine Norrie

DESIGNED BY Parham Santana

First published in 2008 by Girl Scouts of the USA
420 Fifth Avenue, New York, NY 10018-2798
www.girlscouts.org

ISBN: 978-0-88441-714-9

Printed in Italy

2 3 4 5 6 7 8 9/16 15 14 13 12 11 10 09 08

Page 4: Photo by Sandra McIver, Yongin, Korea.
Page 20: Photo by Matthew Pennington, Dhahran, Saudi Arabia.

Excerpt from A ROOM OF ONE'S OWN by Virginia Woolf, copyright 1929 by Houghton Mifflin Harcourt Publishing Company and renewed 1957 by Leonard Woolf, reprinted by permission of the publisher.

Fist-to-Five Consensus-Building adapted from Fletcher, A. (2002). *FireStarter Youth Power Curriculum: Participant Guidebook*. Olympia, Wash.: Freechild Project.

CONTENTS

"I like listening to the girls exchange ideas and gain appreciation for other points of view. I like throwing out ideas and seeing their reaction. It's great to feel like we've made a difference in who they are becoming."

— Christine Tarne, Girl Scout volunteer, Shawnee, Kansas

BUILDING CIRCLES FROM THE INSIDE OUT

For thousands of years, people have gathered in circles to tell stories, perform ceremonies, offer protection, and resolve conflict—all actions aimed at bettering their world. On this journey, Girl Scout Juniors will create a circle of fun and friendship and then reach out—as agents of change—into the larger circle of their community.

From the journey's start to its closing celebration, the girls will move from a deeper understanding of themselves to discovering how powerful they are as a team to realizing the added strength they gain by reaching out in the wider community to take action with its members.

A Growing Web of Power

THE ROOT OF IT ALL

This journey has its roots in community organizing, a process in which people team up around a common idea or concern to act in the best interest of their community and for the common good.

Like all Girl Scout leadership journeys, Agent of Change reflects the Girl Scout leadership philosophy of Discover (understanding self and values), Connect (inspiring and teaming with others), and Take Action (acting to make the world a better place). This sense of power that starts from within each girl and then spirals outward is like a growing web, and you'll notice references to a web throughout the girls' book. (The playful character of the fashion-conscious spider Dez I. Ner—better known as Dez—offers quips and commentary as she weaves her own web of power through the journey.)

As the journey progresses, the girls expand their own web into the community. As they partner with community members to take action, they develop and strengthen leadership skills—and form relationships, often long-lasting and powerful ones. They also tap into planning steps in order to be organized about taking action in the community. Careful planning and organizing lets the girls feel ready to act and makes them more effective as leaders. Your enthusiasm and insight, along with this guide, will ensure a meaningful experience both for the girls and those they meet and team with.

PERFECT TIMING

What makes Girl Scout Juniors ready for the challenge of community organizing? The timing is perfect because Juniors are just beginning to understand that they can make a difference in the world beyond their families, friends, and classrooms. They've moved beyond being helpers in their communities to being ready to be organizers—they can talk and partner with others, expand their world and their worldview, and be part of an effort to change. Most important, *they believe* they can be real contributors to the world.

How the Girls' Book and Your Guide Weave Together

The girls' book also follows a "from the inside out" progression, with chapters on the Power of One, the Power of Team, the Power of Story, and the Power of Community.

Keep in mind that the girls don't need to follow page by page in their book as you present an activity or discussion. Their book is designed so the girls can read it on their own if they want to. It offers plenty for them to do by themselves or in small groups—but they don't need to do everything.

The activities in the sample sessions of this guide are not so strictly divided. For example, the girls begin to explore the Power of Team in Session 2, while they are still delving into the Power of One.

Your guide also includes a few helpful extras, including a sample letter and checklist for the Junior Family and Friends Network. Both of these offer a way to spread the word about the girls' journey and recruit valuable assistance for the girls' Take Action Project. There's also a Take Action Project Checklist that will help you ensure that the girls' Take Action Project focuses on real community change.

ON THEIR OWN

Encourage the girls to enjoy the sidebars and word puzzles that are meant for them to dip into on their own. Remind them that this is their book—theirs to add their thoughts to as they progress along all life's journeys.

CUSTOM FIT

The girls' book and your guide offer a community-mapping exercise and other charts. So decide how they best fit with what interests girls on this journey. Some girls find it easier to think and express their ideas in these visual ways.

The Power of Story

FICTION VS. REALITY

As you engage the girls in the "SuperShelterMakers" story, you will guide them in exploring how to team with others in their community. Remind them that the story is a fictional tale of "supergirls." So, while the girls in the story find success without a hitch, real Take Action Projects may face some challenges.

Dez's main role is as the commentator for "SuperShelterMakers," the comic-book-style story that anchors this journey and engages girls in exploring the difference between one-time service and long-lasting action that gets at the root of a community need.

The journey includes many other stories—contemporary and historic—of girls and women who have reached out to take action in their communities. Through these tales, the Juniors come to understand the power of story and it's role in a community. Stories can come from all types of communities—family, friends, places of worship, cultures, nations—and they are one of the best tools for learning. They help people digest new information, shape their views of the world, and fine-tune their responses to the views of others. Stories can inspire and move people to act, and they can help people face fears with courage.

When a story can actually move the girls to take action in their community, a new story—the Juniors' own story—will begin. The girls will first have a chance to create their own stories on paper, using superheroes and "SuperShelterMakers" as their inspiration. Then, through their Take Action Project, they'll create their own "real-life story." The girls' real-life story will weave together with other stories in the community, and frame those that came before. Most important, their "story" will motivate them to continue taking action to better the world.

"Our stories contain the answers to each others' questions. What I cannot find in searching through the riches and rubble of my own life may become apparent to me in the witnessing of yours."

—Jan Phillips, from *A Waist Is a Terrible Thing to Mind*

You might think of this journey visually as a giant spiral:

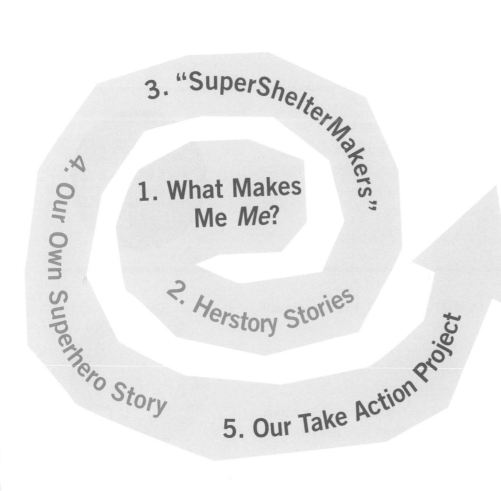

3. "SuperShelterMakers"

4. Our Own Superhero Story

1. What Makes Me *Me*?

2. Herstory Stories

5. Our Take Action Project

STORIES THAT INSPIRE

You can engage the girls in even more stories—and expand their connections to the community around them—by providing opportunities for them to hear from people who are strengthening community in their region. When the girls can hear about someone working through periods of fear and doubt and acting courageously, they will be similarly inspired. The same is true of fictional stories: If the girls feel a story's suspense and the emotions of its characters, there's a good chance they will relate those feelings to their own lives.

Get inspired!
Get artsy with it!
Is your story on a giant roll of paper?
On cardboard strung together?
Show it off!
Who can you tell it...

FRAMED!

what makes me

Awards Along the Journey

The Agent of Change offers girls a chance to earn three awards—the Power of One Award, the Power of Team Award, and the Power of Community Award. In keeping with circular symbols often used to represent community and sharing (and Dez's own spider web), these awards are circular, too—and build on each other from the inside out.

To earn the Power of One Award, girls:

- discover and share the powerful story of a forgotten woman or girl from around the world who mobilized others and made a difference

- use their own "power log" to discover all the ways their strengths and powers help them create change in the world

- discover what the Girl Scout Law and true "heroines" share

To earn the Power of Team Award, girls connect with their Girl Scout crew to:

- create a short "supergirl" story, comic, or TV script in which the characters take one small situation they care about and strive for long-lasting community change

- make a team decision and write their team hopes for a Take Action Project that reaches into a community network to solve a problem together with community members

To earn the Power of Community Award, girls

- take action on their plan, reach out, join others and get them involved, and start something that snowballs into a change in their world

- join in their Girl Scout Junior circle to reflect on what they accomplished and celebrate it

Tracking the Girls' Progress

The Journey Power Award Tracker that begins on page 8 of the girls' book lets the Juniors record their progress throughout the journey. Encourage them to fill it in as they complete each step toward an award. By journey's end, they'll see just how powerful a Girl Scout team and the community can be together.

Three Ceremonies or One Big One?

The girls may want to decide ahead of time whether to have award ceremonies as they earn each award or at the end, to celebrate earning them all.

Power, Connections, and Commitment

In Girl Scouts, power is about acting thoughtfully to make something better. When girls join together to develop and encourage personal skills, they find power both as individuals and as a group. They also gain a personal connection and commitment to their team, and this strengthens their involvement in whatever the team chooses to do.

What If a Girl Misses an Award Step?

Find a way for her to do something similar to what she missed so she can still earn the award with her team. If she misses the day that the team shares its heroine stories, she can partner with another girl and trade stories. If she misses out on creating a superhero story with the team, she can create a new ending or "what if" scenario for it. If she misses some Take Action time, she can take the lead in a follow-up step, such as interviewing those who participated, and then share what she learned.

When girls miss a team meeting, your goal is to assist them in finding ways to have the same learning and growing opportunity—and to understand how they can contribute to the team. Girls may not have the exact same experience but they can each take away new insights, connections, and a sense of accomplishment. As you guide girls through meaningful challenges, you might call on the full team of Juniors to brainstorm together about how girls who miss some steps can best get back on track with the journey.

Tips for Taking Action

The Good of Service and the Power of Action

You'll notice that the girls' book includes a section called "The Good of Service and the Power of Action" (page 66). This details the difference between service and long-lasting action. Don't be overly concerned about making the girls' Take Action Project sustainable (though it's great if it can be!). What's most important is that the girls step through the process of identifying community needs and then move forward with thoughtful planning. They'll brainstorm ways to address those needs by reaching out and meeting others in the community and bringing them into their team. This thoughtful process is what will inspire the girls to strive for lasting change all their lives.

Here are some suggestions for how to approach a Take Action Project with Juniors:

❑ **Emphasize the girls' power.** Invite the girls to experience the power they have—right now—to make a difference in the community.

❑ **Consider local action.** This will minimize any logistical hurdles concerning distance and transportation. Plus, being near home will increase their sense of investment.

❑ **Coach for realistic goals.** At this age, girls can easily be inspired to do great things. As they lay out their goals, they may need your guidance on what is actually doable. Let them know it's OK to focus on accomplishing a short-term action within a long-term goal. Their effort will still be important and can lead to a welcome ripple effect.

❑ **Involve other adults.** Plan ahead to get community members to work alongside the girls in their teams. They can assist as the girls work to get good results from their efforts.

❑ **Aim to build the girls' personal skills,** such as public speaking, team cooperation, writing, and problem-solving. At the same time, look for ways to develop their ability to understand how communities function—and how they, as leaders, can act within their communities to achieve lasting change.

CHECK OUT THE CHECKLIST

There will never be enough time in the day to put all these suggestions into action—but just one or two will aid the girls in their journey toward becoming agents of change. The Take Action Project Checklist on page 19 can help you determine whether the journey is raising the girls' awareness of what it takes to reach out beyond their own circle and partner with a community.

Encourage the girls to:

❑ **Explore possible community issues** by clipping news articles for discussion, identifying the "who, what, where, when, how, and why" of the news.

❑ **Keep their eyes, ears, and minds** open to every aspect of their community for possible Take Action Projects.

❑ **Think about community members** to visit with or invite as guest speakers, so they can get involved in the community early on and are ready to team up with its members when the time comes to Take Action.

IDEAS TO KICK AROUND

A few "Great Ideas" for Take Action Projects are also given on page 74 of the girls' book. Use them as suggestions to get the girls thinking of their own issue and a quality plan for acting on it.

REACHING IN TO REACH OUT

Unlike younger girls, who *explore* community, Girl Scout Juniors will use their leadership skills to become *partners* in the community. It's important for them to meet and talk with people outside their own circle to learn about community strengths and needs. So arrange opportunities for them to engage directly with community members, and create plenty of chances to visit and hear from older Girl Scouts, teens, or inspiring adults who can expand the girls' community network.

TAKE ACTION RESOURCES

You may want to start a Take Action Project Possibilities Bank for the journey so that by Session 4, the girls have access to a variety of resources, such as online news homepages, press releases from community groups, photos of community organizers, and photos of community-minded leaders.

"Truly ours is a circle of friendships, united by our ideals."

—Juliette Gordon Low

Sample Sessions at a Glance

SESSION 1

Discovering My Power

Girls have a chance to see their own strengths and powers in everyday ways and then start comparing them to those of past and present "heroines."

SESSION 2

Great Leaders and Great Teams

Using the knowledge they've gained about the strengths and powers of "heroines," girls connect personal power to the values expressed in the Girl Scout Law. They then explore what power means in girls' lives and in society, and see their power in action. They earn their first award, the Power of Team Award.

SESSION 3

SuperShelter-Makers

Building on their understanding of their own power and the power of past and present women, the girls explore the powers used by a team of fictional girls who, in a comic-book-style story, take action to improve their community. The girls then create their own supergirl story.

SESSION 4

Learn, Listen, Act! Taking Idea to Action

The girls use the power of story to identify what they care about enough to take action on in their own community. They begin to see how, with team power, they can accomplish great things together.

SESSION 5

Ready, Set, Take Action!

Reaching out into the community, the girls gather the tools and resources needed to take action for change, and earn the Power of Team Award.

SESSIONS 6 & 7

Time for the Take Action Project

Combining the Power of Team and the Power of Community, girls do their Take Action Project. Then they take time to reflect on and celebrate the change they have accomplished as they earn their culminating award, the Power of Community Award.

Identifying Journey "Helpers"

Creating a Family and Friends Network

If other parents or creative teens can assist with any journey experiences, by all means enlist their help. You don't have to do it all! Simply use the Junior Family and Friends Network letter and checklist on the following pages to enlarge your network of volunteers.

Welcome!

Dear Junior Family and Friends Network:

Your Girl Scout Junior has joined a team of girls on a journey to create a powerful impact on the community. The girls will explore their strengths and powers, and then, as a team, will plan a project within a community that matters to them. The project has the potential to have a lasting effect on the community.

Your guidance and expertise can help make their experience even more valuable and memorable. Please take a moment to review the attached checklist to let us know which areas you might have expertise in, or time to volunteer for, so that your Junior and her sister Girl Scouts will have the richest experience possible. Then please help your Junior and her team by identifying any areas in which you feel you could contribute time or talent—for the benefit of all Juniors.

The girls and I look forward to hearing from you—and seeing you at sessions throughout the journey.

Sincerely,

JUNIOR FAMILY AND FRIENDS CHECKLIST

YES, I WANT TO HELP THE JUNIORS SUCCEED.

I am ready to volunteer by offering:

☐ ideas about taking action to improve the community

☐ knowledge of issues that interest Girl Scout Juniors

☐ art, building, or craft skills

☐ practical experience with the outdoors

☐ time as a driver (if needed for outings)

☐ time as an all-around Junior leadership journey helper

☐ to bring "powerful" snacks to the session

My Girl Scout Junior's name is: _____

My name: _____

My contact info: _____

YES! I know of community issues and contact people that might interest the Juniors as they choose and do a Take Action Project.

1. _____

2. _____

3. _____

4. _____

5. _____

Take Action Project Checklist

Keep this checklist as a handy reference—especially as the girls progress through their Take Action Project. It will assist you in ensuring that the girls are engaging in a high-quality action. Make some notes, if it's useful, for how you went about accomplishing these important steps.

CHECKPOINT	ACCOMPLISHED BY
Girls identify assets and needs in a community.	
Girls reach out beyond their circle to meet others—people who serve the community and those who might need service.	
Girls make a team decision about what they will take action on.	
Girls learn the steps needed to carry out an action plan.	
Girls partner with others in a community.	
Girls assist with project logistics (transportation requests, the open and close times of organizations, charting team tasks).	
Girls take action alongside community members, joining forces with the community as it moves toward lasting change. (It's important that the girls partner with community members and not see themselves as simply "helping" a community.)	
Girls reflect on their action and assess what they gained from it.	
Girls celebrate their community accomplishments with their partners.	

"**Juniors have so many interests** and are beginning to develop their independence—it really keeps me on my toes! I love encouraging them to create their own opportunities."

—Yvonne Matlosz, Girl Scout volunteer, High Point, North Carolina

YOU AND YOUR GROUP OF GIRL SCOUT JUNIORS

Throughout this journey, you and the girls will gain deeper knowledge of one another and the rich traditions of Girl Scouting. So take some time to understand the likes and needs of Junior-age girls, and then dip into the traditions and ceremonies of Girl Scouts and the "what and how" of creating quality Girl Scout experiences. As you read about the long-lasting leadership benefits of Girl Scouting, think about your own perspective on leadership. Your interest and enthusiasm are sure to be a driving force for the Juniors as they travel through the journey.

Understanding Junior-Age Girls

Your fourth- and fifth-grade "community organizers" are going to expect you to understand who they really are at their age.

Keep in mind that fourth-graders:

Like to please,	*so set expectations high and they will rise to meet them. Yet don't push: Perfectionism is overrated and paralyzes girls. What they learn as they strive toward goals counts most.*
Need groups and clubs,	*so make this experience one in which the girls cooperate and feel a sense of belonging in the group.*
Want to make decisions and express their opinions,	*so give plenty of opportunities for the girls to make group choices.*

And keep in mind that fifth-graders:

Like to develop their talents,	*so expose them to varied activities and choices.*
Need acceptance of their personalities and their styles	*so encourage every girl to be herself.*
Want to do sports, arts and crafts, and put on plays and skits	*so from the start, check out their favorite ways of expressing themselves and find ways to involve each girl's talents. The "Power of Story" section offers lots of way to be creative.*

No matter what grade the Juniors are in:

They're able to see the consequences of mishandling disagreements, *so assist them as they work out conflicts.*

They easily see right from wrong and fair from unfair, *so provide them with opportunities to identify situations that call for ethical decisions—especially as they create their own stories.*

Allow them their sense of "what's right is right" *and help them find ways to change something they interpret as obviously unjust.*

What + How: Creating a Quality Experience

G irl Scouting, it's not just what girls do but *how* you engage them in a girl-adult partnership that will ensure they have a high-quality experience. All Girl Scout activities are built on three processes—Girl Led, Cooperative Learning, and Learning by Doing—that make Girl Scouting unique from school and other extracurricular activities. When used together, these processes ensure the quality and promote the fun and friendship so integral to Girl Scouting.

Take some time to understand these processes and how to apply them with Girl Scout Juniors. (More specific examples of implementing them are woven throughout this guide.)

Girl Led

"Girl led" is just what it sounds like—girls play an active part in figuring out the what, where, when, how, and why of their activities. They lead the planning and decision-making as much as possible. This ensures that girls are engaged in their learning and experience leadership opportunities as they prepare to become active participants in their local and global communities.

With Juniors, this might mean that the girls:

• decide how they want to plan sessions and activities, begin and end meetings, and lead some meetings

• brainstorm possible ways of doing suggested activities—or offer substitutions to make activities more to their taste

• choose their own Take Action Project—one they really care about

• call, interview, and e-mail prospective community members to be guides and assistants on the Take Action Project

KEEP IT GIRL LED

Remember: You want the girls to take a major role in planning and executing this leadership experience. The girls may first want you to come up with the ideas and plans. *But hold your ground!* This is the girls' experience, and they're up to the challenge.

From beginning to end, keep your eye on what the girls want to do and the direction they seem to be taking. It's the approach begun by Juliette Gordon Low: When she and her associates couldn't decide on a new direction, she often said, "Let's ask the girls!" At each session, ask the girls for any last thoughts on what they've done or discussed.

- act *alongside* other adults in the community who have come forward to assist the girls in their action plans

- develop additional ways to research community needs and rehearse phone calls or in-person requests with each other and with you

- select "side trips" for the journey

Learning by Doing

Learning by Doing, also known as Experiential Learning, is a hands-on learning process that engages girls in continuous cycles of action and reflection that result in deeper understanding of concepts and mastery of practical skills. As they participate in meaningful activities and then reflect on them, girls get to explore their own questions, discover answers, gain new skills, and share ideas and observations with others. Throughout the process, it's important for girls to be able to connect their experiences to their lives and apply what they have learned to their future experiences.

Because Junior-age girls are beginning to understand the viewpoints of others, they need opportunities to learn through role-playing, stories, and case studies. This means providing experiences that:

- are hands-on, literally—the girls might work together to make up a TV script, for example, or, on their own, produce a Power Log or a map of their communities

- promote discussion and reflection on what they learned from the "doing" ("How did our team plan and do the project as a group?")

- give the girls time to reflect on how to apply what they have learned to what's next on their journey ("If you could continue doing this project, what would you keep? What would you work out or change?")

CAPTURING THE EXPERIENCE

Rather than racing from activity to activity, give yourself and the girls "permission" for some quiet time to stop, think, talk, and reflect. Encourage a variety of ways to capture the ideas and fun moments of this journey—journaling, sharing in a circle, using clay, paints, or doodling markers—whatever suits the girls.

• encourage the girls to share their points of view and talk about beliefs and values

• provide active experiences to reinforce the activity content, such as ropes courses or trips to places of power in the community: local government, school boards, community action groups

• incorporate ways for you and parents to learn from the girls' reflections on their experiences

To maximize opportunities for letting ideas and experiences sink into the girls' minds and hearts:

• Encourage the girls to write in their books.

• Ask questions that prompt the girls to think about what is important to them, what's working, what may not yet be working.

• Remind the girls to jot down observations or make lists of situations and events that bug them, things they'd like to change.

• Take time for your own reflections, too—it's good modeling for the girls to see.

Cooperative Learning

Through cooperative learning, girls work together toward shared goals in an atmosphere of respect and collaboration that encourages the sharing of skills, knowledge, and learning. Working together in all-girl environments also encourages girls to feel powerful and emotionally and physically safe, and it allows them to experience a sense of belonging even in the most diverse groups.

So give Juniors plenty of:

• opportunities for group projects, which rely on a good spirit of interdependence among the girls

• opportunities to create their own team rules

• encouragement as they begin to see how they can use their power as a group to effect change—in their team and beyond

• guidance as they learn to act as a team within a community

• time to work out their own solutions to problems before you offer your opinion (as long as physical safety isn't at stake)

• time to reflect as a group so they can adapt their plans and determine what to do better next time

Girl Scout Traditions and Ceremonies

For nearly 100 years, Girl Scout traditions and ceremonies have connected girls to each other, to their sister Girl Scouts and Girl Guides around the world, and to generations of Girl Scouts who came before them.

A few Girl Scout traditions are mentioned here; your Girl Scout council will have many more. Try incorporating some of these into Girl Scout gatherings and get-togethers. And don't forget to involve the girls in creating and passing on new traditions.

The Girl Scout Sign

The Girl Scout sign is made when saying the Girl Scout Promise. It is formed by holding down the thumb and little finger on the right hand and leaving the three middle fingers extended (these three fingers represent the three parts of the Promise).

The Girl Scout Handshake

The Girl Scout Handshake is the way many Girl Guides and Girl Scouts greet each other. They shake their left hands while making the Girl Scout sign with their right hand. The left-handed handshake represents friendship because the left hand is closer to the heart than the right.

Widening the Friendship Circle

The Friendship Circle and friendship squeeze is often formed as a closing ceremony for meetings or campfires. Everyone gathers in a circle, crosses their right arm over their left, and holds hands with the people on either side. Once everyone is silent, one girl starts the friendship squeeze by squeezing the hand of the person to the left. One by one, each girl passes on the squeeze until it travels around the circle.

Since this Girl Scout Junior journey emphasizes the power of gathering in a circle, you might widen that concept by inviting a teen to one of your opening or closing ceremonies to share her experiences. And think about inviting a senior citizen to share a memory of a powerful or brave moment in his or her life.

Ceremonies, Step by Step

Why plan a ceremony?

• Something important is about to happen or has happened.

• You want to celebrate big events—a birth, graduations, holidays, etc.

• You want to add something special to everyday events—mealtimes, bedtime, etc.

What do ceremonies do? They:

• Create a space and an atmosphere for gathering with a united purpose.

• Express one big idea or intention by putting it into a frame with a beginning, middle, and end.

• Give the girls opportunities to create rituals around big and small occasions and see them as basic human expressions of togetherness.

Early in the journey, invite the girls to start thinking about how they'd like to celebrate the culmination of this journey together. And along the way, invite them to create as many smaller celebrations as they like. Each time the Juniors gather in their circle can represent a special occasion.

What do ceremonies need?

• **Some planning**—with involvement from the girls

• **Props, reading, music**—to nourish the senses (use diverse selections)

• **Skits or gestures** created for the occasion or to celebrate the spirit of friendship

• **Safety precautions**—candlelight is atmospheric, but flashlights can provide a similar mood (check *Safety-Wise*)

• **Something for each person to do**—no matter how small. These should be real actions, a tangible expression of the ceremony's intention

• **If there will be food**, make it simple and easily shared

• **A clear beginning** that draws the girls together into a circle

• **A distinct closing** with a song, thank you, or handshake

---

FOR MORE CEREMONY IDEAS

Visit www.girlscouts. org/program/gs_central/ ceremonies, or read about traditional Girl Scout ceremonies in *Ceremonies in Girl Scouting* (GSUSA, 1990).

Health, Safety, and Well-Being

CONTACT INFO FOR YOUR GIRL SCOUT COUNCIL

Name:_____

_____

Can help with:_____

_____

_____

_____

Phone: _____

E-mail: _____

_____

The emotional and physical safety and well-being of girls is of paramount importance in the Girl Scout community. Look out for the safety of girls by following *Safety-Wise* when planning all gatherings and trips, and

- checking into any additional guidelines your Girl Scout council might have based on local issues

- talking to girls and their families about special needs or concerns

- creating a safe and trusting emotional space for girls by partnering with them to make and stick to a team agreement

- reminding girls not to disclose their names, addresses, or contact information if they are interacting online

- calling on your council if you need additional expertise or referrals to community resources.

Welcoming Girls with Disabilities

Scouting embraces girls with many different needs at all age levels and is guided by a very specific and positive philosophy of inclusion that benefits all: Each girl is an equal and valued member of a group with typically developing peers.

As an adult volunteer, you have the chance to improve the way society views girls with disabilities. One way to start is with language. Your words have a huge impact on the process of inclusion. People First Language puts the person before the disability.

SAY	INSTEAD OF
She has autism.	She's autistic.
She has an intellectual disability.	She's mentally retarded.
She has a learning disability.	The girl is learning-disabled.
She uses a wheelchair.	She is wheelchair-bound.
She has a disability.	She is handicapped.

Learn What a Girl Needs

Probably the most important thing you can do is to ask the individual girl or her parents or guardians what she needs to make her experience in Girl Scouts successful. If you are frank with and accessible to the girl and her parents, it's likely they will respond in kind, creating a better experience for all.

It's important for all girls to be rewarded based on their best efforts—not completion of a task. Give any girl the opportunity to do her best and she will. Sometimes that means changing a few rules or approaching an activity in a more creative way. Here are a few examples:

• Let a girl perform an activity after observing others doing it first.

• Let the girls come up with ideas on how to adapt an activity.

Often what counts most is staying flexible and varying your approach with the girls.

For a list of online resources, visit www.girlscouts.org and search on "disability resources."

Power Snacks

Enjoying food together is a time-honored, team-building tradition. Plus, the right snacks will give the girls (and adults!) a great energy boost as the journey moves forward. Agent of Change offers a ready-made opportunity to encourage girls to take pleasure in some truly powerful snacks—ones that include protein and fiber (and not too much sugar):

- sliced fruit (such as apples or bananas) with spoonfuls of peanut butter or, even better, almond butter

- low-fat cheese with whole-grain crackers and grapes

- cereal (not the too-sugary kind) with low-fat or skim milk (why not at 4 p.m.?)

- yogurt with fruit or a small amount of granola

- baked chips with a yogurt dip or salsa

- celery stuffed with cream cheese

- almonds and raisins

Always ask about food allergies before anyone serves anything. And find out what mostly-good-for-you treats the Juniors and their families can take turns bringing and sharing.

If you have the time and a few tools, the team might want to whip up fruit shakes (fruit, ice, and skim milk in a blender) on a hot day—or warm up some apple cider on a cold one.

And, as you and the girls explore the community, be on the lookout for snack ideas:

• Is there a farmers' market? What can you make out of what is being sold there?

• Food from around the world? What's powerfully good for you as you "globe trot" locally?

• Book store, health-food store, restaurants? Perhaps a chef can share an easy, tasty, and powerful recipe.

Understanding the Journey's Leadership Benefits

Though filled with fun and friendship, this Junior journey is designed to develop the skills and values girls need to be leaders in their own lives and as they grow.

Girl Scouts of the USA has identified 15 national outcomes, or benefits, of the Girl Scout Leadership Experience. Activities on the Agent of Change journey are designed to enable fourth- and fifth-grade girls to achieve seven of these outcomes, as detailed in the chart on the next page. You can notice the "signs" of these benefits throughout the journey.

Each girl is different, so don't expect them all to exhibit the same signs to indicate what they are learning along the journey. What matters is that you are guiding the Juniors toward leadership skills and qualities they can use right now—and all their lives.

For definitions of the outcomes and the signs that Girl Scout Juniors are achieving them, see the chart on the next page or *Transforming Leadership: Focusing on Outcomes of the New Girl Scout Leadership Experience* (GSUSA, 2008). Keep in mind that the intended benefits to girls are the cumulative result of traveling through an entire journey—and everything else girls experience in Girl Scouting.

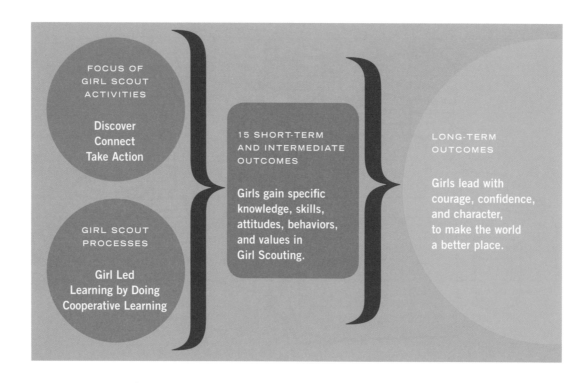

FOCUS OF GIRL SCOUT ACTIVITIES

**Discover
Connect
Take Action**

GIRL SCOUT PROCESSES

**Girl Led
Learning by Doing
Cooperative Learning**

15 SHORT-TERM AND INTERMEDIATE OUTCOMES

Girls gain specific knowledge, skills, attitudes, behaviors, and values in Girl Scouting.

LONG-TERM OUTCOMES

Girls lead with courage, confidence, and character, to make the world a better place.

NATIONAL LEADERSHIP OUTCOMES

		AT THE JUNIOR LEVEL, girls...	RELATED ACTIVITIES	SAMPLE "SIGN" When the outcome is achieved, girls might...
DISCOVER	**Girls develop a strong sense of self.**	gain a clearer sense of their individual identities in relation to and apart from outside influences.	"What Makes Me *Me*?" (Session 1) "The GS Law Meets the Heroine in Me" (Session 2)	report increased confidence in dealing with outside pressures that try to dictate their thoughts and behaviors (e.g., peer pressure, advertising, cultural traditions).
	Girls develop critical thinking skills.	show greater skill in gathering and evaluating information.	"Rediscovering *Her*story" (Session 1); "Who Can Mobilize the Moxie?" (Session 2); "Building Consensus: Fist-to-Five" (Session 4)	consider various factors before deciding what to believe (e.g., how credible was the source of information, is there a hidden agenda?).
CONNECT	**Girls promote cooperation and team building.**	are better able to initiate and maintain cooperation on their teams.	All activities in Sessions 2–4	with minimal adult guidance, apply specific strategies for promoting cooperation (e.g., listening to all ideas, rotating tasks and roles, developing shared goals).
	Girls feel connected to their communities, locally and globally.	are better able to recognize the importance of knowing about and actively participating in their community groups.	"Defining Community" (Session 4); Doing the project (Sessions 5–7)	identify various sources of information for what is going on in their communities (e.g., the Internet, magazines, interviews with people).
TAKE ACTION	**Girls can identify community needs.**	learn to use strategies to determine issues that deserve action.	"Narrow It Down"; "Campaign for Change"; (Session 4)	use community asset mapping to identify opportunities to better their communities.
	Girls are resourceful problem solvers.	are better able to create an "action plan" for their projects.	"Who's Going to Do What?" "Take Action Project Checklist" (Session 5)	outline steps, resources, and time lines and assign responsibilities for their project with minimal adult guidance.
	Girls feel empowered to make a difference.	are more confident in their power to effect positive change.	Sessions 6 and 7	describe various expressions of power around them (e.g., power over others, power to do something, power with others).

Your Perspective on Leadership

The Girl Scout Leadership philosophy—Discover + Connect + Take Action—implies that leadership happens from the inside out. It stresses the importance of embracing who you are, connecting with others, and working collaboratively to make things better for *all*.

As you read through the Girl Scout Junior journey, think about your own view of leadership from the inside out. You and the girls will have a richer experience if you can use your own reflections as part of how you inspire the girls to feel empowered to make a difference in the world.

Take a few minutes now to apply the three keys of leadership to yourself by using the following reflection, which you can revisit throughout the journey:

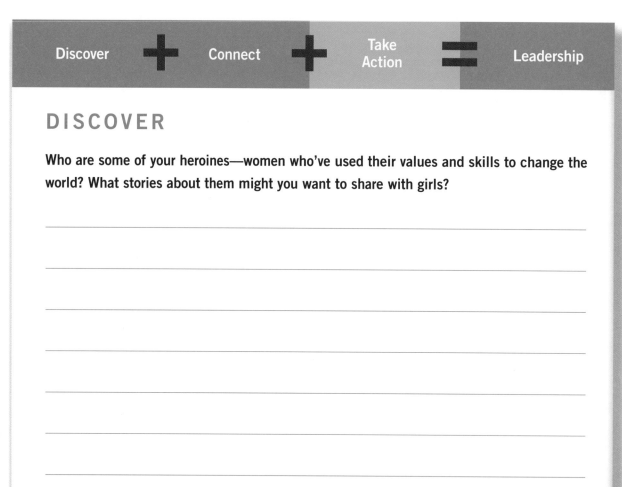

| Discover | **+** | Connect | **+** | Take Action | **=** | Leadership |

DISCOVER

Who are some of your heroines—women who've used their values and skills to change the world? What stories about them might you want to share with girls?

What values and skills—your own powers—make you uniquely you? How do you use them "from the inside out"? How will this influence your efforts to guide girls to explore the Power of One?

_____

_____

_____

_____

_____

_____

_____

CONNECT

What is the best experience you have ever had being on a team?

_____

_____

_____

_____

What did team members do to make it great?

_____

_____

_____

_____

What will you bring from this experience of true belonging to guide girls to experience the Power of Team?

_____

_____

_____

_____

How do your connections to different communities enrich your life?

_____

_____

_____

_____

How can you assist girls to expand their connections to community?

_____

_____

_____

_____

TAKE ACTION

As a Girl Scout volunteer, you are part of the Power of Community—people making the world a better place. Why does this matter to you? How will the girls experience this Power of Community?

_____

_____

_____

_____

_____

_____

_____

_____

_____

_____

_____

_____

_____

_____

"With Juniors, you explain what you want them to do and then step back and watch in wonder. They never cease to amaze me with what they are willing to take on."

—Cathy Brookes, Girl Scout volunteer and alumna, Frederick, Maryland

THE JOURNEY'S 7 SAMPLE SESSIONS

Think of the session plans in this guide as a basic road map—they'll take you and the girls through each step of the journey, accomplishing goals along the way. Each session is designed to allow the girls to make choices so that the journey is as meaningful and memorable as possible.

Each session could run 60 to 90 minutes following this basic plan:

- an opening ceremony or simple gathering (about five minutes, although the first opening might take 10-15 minutes)
- activities that open the girls' involvement in the session's purpose—sometimes beginning with brainstorming and discussion; at other times starting with an energizing activity
- activities to get further into the session's purpose—any of which can be shortened or lengthened or cut, depending on what you and the girls decide
- reflection time—if possible, devote five minutes to this in every session
- closing ceremony (when you want one)

Tips for Working with the Sample Sessions

NEED TO SCALE BACK? JUST STAY FOCUSED!

If you are limited to 6–8 sessions, keep in mind that you don't have to do every activity. You'll get the most out of each one by keeping it small in scale and focused. If possible, allow for Sessions 6 and 7 to be longer so that the girls have the time they need to engage in the action they plan.

KEEP IT GIRL LED

Let any ideas that the girls latch on to take them in the direction *they'd* like to go. For instance, the girls may want to extend the power log, word games, or the "Flip the Script" activity. These kinds of things will keep the sessions fresh and girl led.

f the Juniors' time for this journey is not limited to 6–8 sessions—or you have more time at some sessions—you will be able to expand these key journey activities:

*Her*story: As girls find and then share with one another the stories of powerful heroines, past or present, they can share them with a wider circle. That may mean other Junior teams, younger Girl Scouts, or older Girl Scouts (who can share their own ideas with the Juniors). Or the Juniors might create an exhibit of their heroine stories for a local library, school, or other community location.

Power Story: Girls can take their time creating their story and then decide how to share it with a larger circle. They might even display it for others to see.

Take Action Project: If the girls expand their *Her*story and Power Story time, they may not start their Take Action Project until Session 6 or so—or even 8 or 9! At that point, they will be deciding on their project, and then planning and doing it for the remainder of the journey—which could stretch out to eight or even 10 sessions or maybe 12!

So, there's no need to rush through and do everything in seven meetings. You could even add an additional session—or two—between Sessions 3 ("SuperShelterMakers") and 4, where the girls get started on their Take Action Project. Or, if the girls are not so interested in that, keep that part of the journey smaller and jump into the Take Action Project sooner. Just be sure to let the girls' time and interest shape whatever route you choose.

Detours Along the Journey

And if you and your "travelers" have time, be imaginative. Ask the girls how and when they'd like to get "off the highway" to stop at their own "roadside attractions." They might want to add on:

Story stuff: opportunities to experience how stories of all kinds are created and shared—whether plays (organize a trip to the theater!), films, books (writing, illustration, and design), photo essays, art exhibits, oral histories.

Trips to research various parts of the girls' communities. Encourage the girls to jot down their observations. Sometimes the best project is right in their own backyard—the nearest playground, library, food pantry, or nursery school. Even a trip to the mall can spark the girls' imaginations to come up with new ideas.

Outdoor (or indoor) activities that offer plenty of physical activity. If not enough are suggested in this guide, create some of your own—even if not elaborate.

Ask the girls what they enjoy—perhaps classics like tag, time to go a little crazy while listening to music, or a jumping-jacks break—and where they like to go. Their favorite places may be good spots to take the girls for a break, and they may be places that the girls want to improve in some way.

Simply getting out from time to time for a walk, a picnic, or to practice map reading and compass skills will also be welcome. The Juniors might even like to try a themed hike:

- to collect items from nature for collages. (Thought for the hike: Is there any way we can protect the trees in our area?)
- to find elements of the water cycle—snow or fog; run-off water; bodies of water or flowing water. (Thought for the hike: How much water do we waste when we brush our teeth with the water running?)

Crafts: And, if girls express interest, encourage arts and crafts opportunities as they arise. Several discussions or activities can easily be extended into craft projects. For instance, after the girls complete their "Power Logs," some may want to make "power bracelets" to trade with one another—it keeps the "circle" theme going. Craft projects can also become mementos that the girls will keep in their books or incorporate into ceremonies.

OUT AND ABOUT WITH ANIMALS

Most girls love animals, so the puppies in "SuperShelterMakers" might inspire them to get up-close and personal with animals. Here are a few ideas:

- Organize an outing that lets the girls observe animals in their natural habitat. (Remind the girls not to disturb any plants or animals they might see.)

- Visit an animal shelter, a zoo, or farm—whatever your community offers. (Even if you live in a congested urban area, there's bound to be a park with birds, insects, and squirrels—all of which can be observed to learn their "story.")

If visiting a natural habitat, ask the girls how it might change with the seasons. (Consider visiting more than once so girls can observe the changes.)

No matter where they go, encourage the girls to draw pictures or maps of the area they visit.

SAMPLE SESSION 1
Discovering My Power

AT A GLANCE

Goal: Girls discover their own values and individual "powers" by looking at their daily activities and sharing in the stories of others.

- Opening Ceremony
- Thinking About Power
- What Makes Me *Me*? Or, I'm Being Framed!
- Power Log
- Looking Back at *Her*story and Dream Team Trading Cards

MATERIALS

- Long rope
- Large sheet of paper (taped on wall so the rope can be pinned or taped to the paper in any shape the girls want)
- Index cards
- List of the Girl Scout Law qualities (use the list on the inside front cover or make your own list)
- Power log (see page 8–9 in the girls' book)
- Markers
- Paper
- Scissors

ADVANCE PREP

Read over the section "Don't Forget to Celebrate" on page 30 of the girls' book.
It's a good reminder of how effective it is to gather the girls in a circle for a quick
mood-setting or reflection time. Or come up with your own ways to use circles to
build a sense of community among the girls.

Circles are key to Girl Scout ceremonies—from Friendship Circles and squeezes
to the simple act of meeting in a circle. The circle invites the girls away from
everyday distractions and offers meaningful face-to-face interaction.

Of course, you may not want to have both an opening and closing ceremonies
at each session. Consider alternating the two—an opening ceremony at one, a
closing at the next.

KEEP IT GIRL LED

Encourage the girls to assist in planning and carrying out opening and closing
ceremonies (see ideas for ceremonies on pages 30–31 of the girls' book).

The values of the Girl Scout Promise and Law, which have been the cornerstone
of Girl Scouting for nearly a century, might serve as a focal point for ceremonies.
Girl Scouts of every age are encouraged to discover these qualities in themselves
in order to be leaders. You might invite girls to say the Promise and Law together,
or choose one line and invite each girl to say what it means to her.

Opening Ceremony

As the girls begin their journey, mark the importance of this big event in the lives of Juniors with a ceremony—either the one described here or another from your Girl Scout council.

Begin with a rope long enough to extend around the circle of girls in your group. Tie one knot on the rope for each girl to hold as they all stand in a circle. Gather the girls in a circle and hold the knot at one end of the rope, letting the rest of the rope hang on the floor. After you speak, you will pick up the next knot and pass it to the girl next to you. She will hold a knot, speak, and then pass the knot to the next girl. Modify this ceremony as you like.

Say something like:

> *I invite you to introduce yourself and tell us why you are here today. I'll begin:*
>
> *I want to be called _____. I am here today because I want to be with you in this circle of friendship.*
>
> *And I want to be with each of you as we start our journey in a friendly and brave way to change the world—starting with our community.*
>
> *We're passing around this rope and telling our reasons for joining this group. Think of this rope as a sturdy thread linking us with all Girl Scouts, and our sister Girl Guides, as well as girls all around the world.*

After the rope has gone around and the girls have introduced themselves, pass out the index cards. Ask the girls to:

1. Pin or tape the rope to the large sheet of paper in any shape they choose.

2. Write their names beneath the knot they held.

3. Write on their index card one to three qualities from the Girl Scout Law that they would like to discover in themselves during this leadership journey. Pin or tape each girl's card on the paper beneath her name. The girls can revisit this "rope poster" of index cards at the end of the journey and assess how far they've come in discovering their qualities.

If you wish, gather in a circle again and close by saying the Girl Scout Promise and Law.

"Girl Scouting can be the magic thread which links the youth of the world together."

—Juliette Gordon Low

Future Ceremonies

Before breaking up the circle, ask the girls to think of ways they would like to gather in a circle for future ceremonies. They may want to come up with some variations on the rope ceremony by adding on one new element each time they meet. Suggest that small groups could plan and take the lead in creating an opening or closing ceremony for any session. Have a sign-up list for girls to take turns planning a ceremony. Having girls take an active role in the opening and closing ceremonies is a great way to ensure a girl-led experience!

Throughout the sessions, girls will gain inspiration from looking at role models, past and present and near and far. If you like, preview the bios of role models in the girls' book (pages 18–22 and 27). Offer up role models you like, too—past and present.

Thinking About Power

The girls' book opens with "The Journey: What It's All About," which presents a discussion of what "power" is. Chapter 2, "The Power of One," moves into a discussion of what some of the girls' own particular powers are. Engage the Juniors in a discussion by using the statements about power in their book as prompts.

- Ask the girls if they agree or **disagree** with the statements.

- If they disagree, ask them for reasons and explanations. (Remind them that it's OK to have and share differing opinions.)

- Then, reinforce that **expressing an opinion is a powerful act—and they've accomplished it.** That's another power that the girls can add to their list!

ME TIME: IT'S A GOOD THING!

Girls need time, and often the suggestion, to think and write about themselves, especially when it comes to their talents and powers. At first they might say, "I don't have any talents." But give them the time, and you'll notice more thought creeping into what they have to say. Something as simple as journaling can help clarify their feelings.

ANITA BAKER'S QUOTE

The quote from jazz artist Anita Baker is displayed prominently in the girls' book. Many girls may not have heard of Anita Baker, so let them know that in the world of jazz music she's been a leader for decades. She also determined the course of her own career. Here are some prompts to start a discussion with the girls:

What does it mean to be an independent thinker? Why are independent thinkers quick to put their ideas into action?

Why do we sometimes let others make choices for us? What happens when we make our own choices?

What Makes Me *Me*?
Or, I'm Being Framed

This activity, on page 13 of the girls' book, lets each Junior create a self-portrait collage by combining a picture of herself with words she feels describe her.

Start with a brainstorm. Ask for adjectives that describe the qualities of different people. Use those in the girls' book as a starting point. Ask the girls to write down words that describe themselves, too.

The framed self-portrait in the center of the collage represents the girl's own unique space. (If girls don't have a photo, invite them to draw their own likeness—literal or abstract—in the frame.) Girls can also add photos of their loved ones, friends, and interests. If any girls want to go all out, they might make their collage outside of their book—from cardboard, recycled materials, words cut from magazines, and the like. If the team has time, you could encourage the girls to spend a whole session on this. Or they could do it at home and share it with the group at a future session. Either way, encourage the girls to be proud of their creations.

Power Log

Girls focus on the powers needed to get through the day by keeping a log of their daily activities and the power they used for them. (See page 15 of the girls' book.) In keeping their logs, the girls will realize that every day they use valuable life skills and powers that call for leadership and teamwork. The Juniors can write their logs in this session or simply start them and bring them back to Session 2. *Either way, make sure the girls recognize how many powers they rely on in one day!*

KEEP IT GIRL LED

Would the girls like to showcase their collages? Some options:

• Invite the girls to work together to plan and set up a gallery exhibit of their work. Begin it now and keep adding to it for the journey's final celebration (where you can also display their *herstories* and power stories, and items from their Take Action Project).

• The girls can set up their own "meet and greet" where they introduce themselves to each other as they mill around the "party" and shake hands. A variation: The girls pose as each other at the meet and greet, using the collages as their scripts for introducing another girl.

• If the girls already know one another, invite each one to tell something new about herself during the meet and greet.

Completing the Power Log is part of earning the first badge of this journey—the Power of One Award.

Once the power logs are complete, ask the girls to share them with the group. Start a discussion by selecting various events and experiences and pointing out what "power" each required. For instance, making a schedule with a parent may have involved *negotiation*, *communication*, and *time management*—as well as *listening*. Extend the discussion to talk about heroines or leaders the girls know—what they do and the powers they exhibit on a given day.

Quotes from prominent women, like the one below, show the girls that there have always been women leaders. (For girls who love to do research, this would be a great door to a project on Juliette Gordon Low.)

KEEP IT GIRL LED

If the girls feel that it would be more fun to create one big team power log, let them dictate the materials and "rules." Then they can brainstorm, plan, and organize the activity. If they'd prefer to keep their power logs private, that's an option, too.

"The work of today is the history of tomorrow, and we are its makers. So let us strive to show just as grand names on the pages yet unwritten as are inscribed on those that we have for our proud inheritance."

—Juliette Gordon Low

Looking Back at *Her*story

During this session, get girls thinking outside the box about women heroines. Start off with a look at the women and girls in the *Her*story and Dream Team sections of their book (page 17–19 and 20–22), and the "moxie" girls (page 27). Then have the girls make a team decision about how and when they will select their heroine:

- On their own or in pairs?

- Between sessions or, if you have computers or other research materials available, during a session?

- Or will they take a team trip to a historical society or library, or invite guest speakers from the community—maybe a local woman leader to talk about what obstacles she has overcome, or perhaps even teen girls?

Keep in mind: The girls might also find their heroine by talking to their mothers, aunts, and teachers.

The goal here is not to create a hefty book report but to discover lesser-known women who will inspire the girls to broaden their view of women's accomplishments. Local women who are active in the community are good candidates; so are Girl Scouts who have earned the Gold or Silver Award.

To get the girls started, share this story template with them or devise your own:

KEEP IT GIRL LED

Underlying this activity may be nagging questions: Why aren't more women well known? And why does this matter? Who or what prevented women from being better known for what they did? Let reactions to these questions trigger a discussion. The girls may also want to discuss how women are viewed now compared to in the past. Allow them to voice their opinions, too—such self-expression is in keeping with becoming a leader.

This is a story of _____ .

Not too many people know about her because _____ .

Her ability to _____ interests me because

_____ .

Here are a few facts about her life:

_____

Next, invite the girls to make a team choice about how they want to share their *her*stories with each other:

- Will they each simply write their story down on paper and share it, or will they make trading cards (see page 20 in the girls' book) or create a work of art that they can display? Let the girls decide whether and how they'll share their stories with a wider circle.

- They might put them together to create a team *her*story 'zine or a huge collage.

- Whatever the format, the result can be shared with others—younger girls, schools, libraries, their Girl Scout council.

- Of course, all this also depends on how much time overall you and the girls have. The girls can go all out with their creativity if the group wants to spend more time on *Her*story.

Completing the *Her*story experience— exploring and sharing stories of heroines— is a step toward the Power of One Award.

GO ALL OUT WITH THE STORY

If time permits, the Juniors might want to exhibit their superhero stories or share them with younger girls.

The girls may enjoy doing some story-making on an overnight; a council camp could be a great place to make the Dream Team Cards (see page 20 in the girls' book) or to really get creative with the superhero story.

FINDING TIME TO EXPLORE *HER*STORY

If you have the time, devote Session 2 to group efforts to find heroines together. Then simply push all the other sessions back one. If the girls prefer individual research time during Session 2, you can still push all the other sessions back as well, or simply move the *her*story-related activities of Session 2 to a later date.

COSTUME PARTY, ANYONE?

The girls might want to schedule a day to wear the costumes of a period in history when a chosen heroine lived. Or mix it up and have each girl dress in the period of her heroine.

Dream Team Trading Cards

Trading Cards, like those on page 20 of the girls' book, offer one creative way to use the discoveries the Juniors make about girls and women, past and present. They reinvent ordinary "trading cards" by focusing on historical or modern heroines. Completing two or three dream team cards is an alternate way to fulfill the award requirement.

When discussing the trading cards with the girls, call attention to each card's list of accomplishments—all come from taking action. Note that each card includes a quote—these women put their words into actions.

If making trading cards, the girls might choose to include their mom, grandmother, teacher—or their Girl Scout volunteers!

SELF-DISCOVERY AND TEAM SPIRIT

For some added fun, encourage the girls to make trading cards about themselves. This is a good way to kick up the team spirit.

You might even suggest that the girls make cards throughout the year—as a way to think about how they might be growing as they gain new skills and powers throughout the journey. They can even glue their new card over their existing one—a symbolic way of building upon their earlier selves.

BEGIN A GROUP GLOSSARY

Include words from the journey, such as mobilize, power, decision-maker—some of which the girls will be introduced to during the next session. Be creative—girls don't necessarily think in ordinary vocabulary. Add made-up words, phrases, short word-memories, and anything else that seems to resonate with the girls. The girls can share their full list as part of their end-of-journey celebration.

Any new power words come to mind?

_____

_____

_____

"For most of history, Anonymous was a woman."

—Virginia Woolf
English novelist and essayist, 1882–1941

Anonymous Was a Woman is now the name of a New York-based foundation that awards grants to women over 40, to enable them to continue to grow and pursue their work at a critical juncture in their lives or careers.

Preparing for Session 2

This session is designed so that the girls can devote a good chunk of it to sharing their *her*stories and having fun with the obstacle course. Given the variety of other activities suggested, perhaps have the girls vote on which they most want to engage in as a group. They can always save any extra activities for later sessions.

*Her*stories

Depending on how girls are exploring their *her*stories (either as a team during a session or on their own), think ahead about how much time you will need during the session so that girls can fully share their stories.

Obstacle Course

You'll need items such as tables to climb over and under, chairs to step up and down from, boxes to step around, and a "footpath" of books to walk across. Use your imagination and work with what you have on hand. Perhaps you can connect with a few girls between sessions and see if they can help. A parent or teen could also help organize how the girls want to set up the obstacles. The "course" could also have some "active stations" where girls do 10 jumping jacks and then hop through, or around, various items. You'll also need one blindfold.

KEEP IT GIRL LED

Setting up the obstacle course is part of the fun—and builds teamwork and decision-making skills, too. So be sure to let the girls lead the way. It also lets the girls finally "move the furniture" and take control of the space they're in (a rare treat for fourth- and fifth-graders).

TAKE IT OUTSIDE

An outdoor obstacle course can be loads of fun. In a camp setting, try similar trust experiences with low-ropes courses or top roping. Check *Safety-Wise* for correct and safe procedures.

me to the MAX

Serena and Venus Williams, athletes

Katherine "Kerry" Close, National Spelling Bee champion

Mark Bowen/Scripps National Spelling Bee

LOOKING BACK AT
*HER*STORY

Did you know . . .

• Until about 500 years ago, women were rarely credited for their inventions, cooking, art, or writing.

• Few of women's courageous contributions to society were recognized.

• Except in the case of a few members of royalty, the works left behind were simply labeled "Unidentified" or "Anonymous."

• It didn't matter how hard they tried or how big they dreamed—early women were often forgotten in the pages of history.

SAMPLE SESSION 2
Great Leaders and Great Teams

AT A GLANCE

Goal: By sharing their "*her*story" with the team, girls explore how powerful individual women have been throughout history. The girls then explore how their own individual powers can be linked together to create a powerful team. They also begin to see how power, leadership, and teamwork connect to the Girl Scout Law.

- Opener
- Getting Back to *Her*story
- Who Led the Way for You?

- Real Powers, Real Girl Scouts
- Trust Me! (obstacle course)
- Closing Ceremony: Real Girls, Real Moxie

AS GIRLS ARRIVE

Suggest that the girls do the "Power Skills, Power Words" puzzle on page 26 of their book as they come in and get settled.

MATERIALS

- Long rope
- Objects for obstacle course
- Cloths for blindfolds

- Optional items for obstacle course: chairs, books,
- boxes, table, etc.

Getting Back to *Her*story

Based on the team's decision in Session 1, have girls read/share/show/trade their "*her*story." Or, if you've added in more time to the journey, this may be when the girls research their *her*stories—they may be doing online research, interviewing a local heroine, or hearing from some "heroine" guest speakers.

Whatever form their "*her*story" investigation takes, the girls will discover that through the centuries, women have accomplished far more than they might have known. And as they use their skills and powers to bring overlooked women into focus, the girls will also begin to think about how their own lives today can offer so much more power than the lives of women centuries, or just decades, earlier.

Start a discussion by asking the girls to define *heroine*:

• *Ask the girls for names of movie stars, celebrities, and other notable women.*

• *Ask: What other heroines do you know?*

• *Explain that some people are known for what they accomplish; others for being rich or beautiful.*

• *Ask: What are your heroines known for?*

Once the girls have shared their *her*stories with the full team, circle back to a group discussion. Encourage the girls to see how being a heroine differs from simply being famous. Ask the girls:

> *Were you surprised by what you learned about your heroines?*

> *Have you discovered that women have been doing many more great things than you realized?*

When the discussion winds down, review the decision the girls made in Session 1 about whether they want to turn their *her*stories into a team collection. If the girls are excited about sharing beyond their own circle, have them finalize their plans.

What format will their collection take—collage, trading cards, 'zine? When will they do the creating? Who will they share them with—other Juniors in their region (if the girls live in an urban area, perhaps they might share them with a group of rural Juniors)? Where will they show them—at a library, an art exhibit, a school display or assembly? Or perhaps the girls want to show them off at their culminating celebration, where they can share all the highlights of their journey.

WHAT? A GIRL WITH NO *HER*STORY?

If any girls have trouble settling on a woman for their *her*story, or they arrive without a *her*story, have a few on hand as suggestions. Here are four possibilities:

Wangari Maathai, the Nobel Peace Prize winner who used the simple idea of planting trees to create the Green Belt Movement in Kenya. By planting trees, poor women in rural villages combat soil erosion, improve water resources, provide wood fuel for cooking, and earn income from forestry. Wangari has helped women plant more than 20 million trees on their farms and on lands around schools and churches.

Alice Waters, the California chef and restaurant owner who reinvented the meaning of school lunch by creating the Edible Schoolyard project that has students raising crops, cooking food, and learning about sustainable ecosystems.

Jane Goodall, the foremost authority on chimpanzees who now devotes her time to nature conservation and environmental education around the world.

Luisa Moreno, who assembled the first national Latino congress for civil rights and was unstoppable in her advocacy for poor immigrants, especially Mexican Americans in Southern California.

Who Led the Way for You?

If the group has time, try this activity from page 28 of the girls' book. Ask the girls to write down the names of their favorite leaders. Encourage the girls to go beyond the obvious answers to other possibly less-recognized leaders.

Then talk about what it means to lead:

- Is it really an individual activity? (No.)

- Does it mean the leader has to be the only authority and make all the decisions? (No.)

When asked, "Who is a leader," the girls may say what they think is expected of them, such as:

- the president

- the school principal

- a sports figure or entertainer

WHAT ABOUT BAD QUALITIES?

The girls may opt to make this an activity about the bad qualities of some leaders and teams. Let them. It can be fun to have a "dissing" session—as long as it's not personal.

Real Powers, Real Girl Scouts

This activity gets the girls thinking about the connections between the values of the Girl Scout Law and the powers it takes to achieve heroic actions.

This activity is the final step to earning the Power of One Award. It strengthens the girls' understanding of how the Girl Scout Law builds the kind of powers real-life heroines need.

Ask the girls to form small teams to find and talk about a quality within the Girl Scout Law that fits one of the heroines they researched. Encourage the girls to explain how the heroine shows a specific value from the Girl Scout Law and then give the girls time to share what they found with the full group.

IT'S ALL ABOUT TEAMWORK

You are inviting girls into an obstacle course to bring to life how individual strengths create an even stronger team. This cooperative learning experience brings the girls together immediately into a team atmosphere where they collaborate on a project and gain from one another's efforts.

Trust Me!

Let the girls know that it's now time for a physical activity about the importance of trust and teamwork—running an obstacle course. The girls will take turns wearing a blindfold and making their way through the course as the rest of the team members call out directions.

Start with a short discussion about the connection between good leadership and good teamwork. Using pages 34–35 in the girls book as a starting point, talk about the nature of good leaders and good teams. What kind of teams can they think of? Sports teams are obvious, but there can be action-taking teams, too. Offer some hints: *A good team is effective, cooperative, considerate, dedicated.*

Then, get started with the obstacle course. As the game unfolds, encourage the girls to take mental notes on what works and what doesn't, so they're ready when it's their turn to wear the blindfold.

After all the girls have had a chance to try the course, take some time to reflect. Some ideas for discussion might include:

- What makes the direction givers' job hard?

- What happens if the direction givers can't imagine what it's like to be the one wearing the blindfold—the one who has to follow the directions? Why is that important?

- How do the two work together?

Closing Ceremony: Real Girls, Real Moxie

This closing underscores just what women are made of—powers, skills, and can-do attitudes!

First, make sure the girls are clear on what "moxie" is. Point them to the definitions given in their books on pages 7 and 25. Moxie means energy, pep, courage, determination, know-how, and expertise—sometimes all rolled into one. A person full of moxie is one who has a lot of spirit mixed with skillfulness.

(Another word for moxie might be *guts*.)

Now, go around the circle and ask each girl to name her favorite superhero and the kind of moxie that hero has. In other words, is it her superpowers or her personality and personal qualities that make her a heroine?

Once each girl has had a chance to answer, ask the full group one last question:

How about teams with moxie? Can you think of any? (Perhaps the girls will be ready to name their own Girl Scout team.)

READING AHEAD

If they're interested, encourage the girls to read the comic-book story "SuperShelterMakers," which will be the focus of Session 3 (unless you have built in an additional session for *her*story activities).

Also, ask the girls to bring a variety of art supplies to the next session—paper, poster board, pens, colored markers—anything they might want to use to create their own comic-book story. These don't need to be new—leftovers can be lots of fun and spark creativity. Have them think about the type of story they might want to create. Will it be big or a small flip-it size? The girls can bring art supplies to fit their format.

SAMPLE SESSION 3
SuperShelterMakers

AT A GLANCE

Goal: The girls find role models and learn the steps for teaming up and taking action—by reading a comic-book story about how a group of girls seized an opportunity, acted on it as a team in a planned way, and involved their community in the project

- Opening Ceremony
- Reading "SuperShelterMakers"
- Begin Your Own Heroine Story
- Closing

MATERIALS

- Paper, poster board, cardboard, colored markers, pens, and whatever else the girls need to make their Superhero stories. (See Reading Ahead note on page 59.) Nothing fancy is needed. Working from odds and ends that everyone brings and shares can be fun!

Opening Ceremony

If girls are earning the Power of One Award, you may want to start with the awards ceremony. Or you may even want to do a traditional Girl Scout opening, such as the flag ceremony. For the details of opening with a flag ceremony or to find a ceremony planner to help in creating your ceremony, visit www.girlscouts.org/program/gs_central/ceremonies/flag.asp.

Reading "SuperShelterMakers"

"SuperShelterMakers" is a story of a few Girl Scouts who have the moxie to mobilize themselves, other girls, and finally a whole community.

Feel free to add your own ideas about "the power of reading" to Dez's "pitch."

Have fun reading the comic-book story. Even if some or all of the girls have read it between sessions, try to have a shared reading experience of the story by:

- asking the girls to volunteer to take the parts—and don't forget Dez's part

- allowing some girls to be on Dez's team and offer responses to Dez's questions along the way

- staying sensitive to the girls' reading skills

Take as long as this activity needs. Let the girls have fun experiencing the story together (which is different from reading it alone—no matter how enjoyable that is).

Begin Your Own Heroine Story

Talk informally about the "SuperShelterMakers" story—whatever in it interests the girls:

- Is there a character they especially like? Why?

- Is there anything they'd do differently?

- What do they think of Dez and her comments?

- What could have gone wrong?

- What "what ifs" can girls think of? How would they solve them?

TEAMWORK IN ACTION

An important element of teamwork is to be able to see another's perspective. Reading "SuperShelterMakers" as a group and then making a story together as a team calls for seeing and acknowledging various points of view.

Ask the girls for their preference: What format do they want their story to take? They can also create their story in small groups or as one large group. One way to start is to answer the "Think About It" questions related to "SuperShelterMakers" on page 67 of the girls' book. Give the girls the time they need to develop their stories in their own way.

Remember, too, that part of the joy of creating a story is the chance to tell it. Who can they tell it to? Other Juniors in the region? Younger girls? Perhaps they want to show it at their school or save it for sharing at their ending celebration.

This activity is part of earning the Power of Team Award.
The girls will form teams to create their own supergirl comic-book story or script, or any kind of visual story about taking action to make their world better. It could be a mini-play, like a TV episode, or a crazy map, a radio show, or a puppet show. Big or small, the choice is up to the girls.

TIME FOR 'TOONS

Time permitting, you and the girls might want to get together—even for a sleepover—to watch cartoons and talk about superheroes. What do heroes have in common? How are girl characters portrayed in the cartoons? What makes them fun to watch? What seems to happen in every episode? Is there a pattern going on that the girls can use as a formula for their own superhero stories?

"There are some things you do alone, but generally speaking, the ones you work on with others are more fun."

—Juliette Gordon Low

Learn, Listen, Act!
Taking Idea to Action

AT A GLANCE

Goal: The girls discuss and decide on an issue that they care about and that is meaningful enough for their community to take action on. Along the way, they also come to understand the importance of consensus to a team.

- **Stories and Their Issues**
- **Defining Community**
- **Building Consensus: Fist-to-Five**
- **The Real Me**
- **Closing Ceremony (optional)**

Keep the Story Going

Based on your group's schedule and time, you may want to use this session for the girls to continue making their own superhero stories and/or sharing them with the team and others. If the girls are excited about what they're creating, give them more time. There's no need to rush.

Stories and Their Issues

As the girls finish their own stories and share them, they can use the issues in those stories to think about taking real action in the real world. Get a discussion going about the various issues the girls put into their stories. Ask:

- *What issues did you create your story about?*

- *Why did you choose these issues?*

- *So many decisions and actions went into your story. What were some of the most important ones?*

- *Who from the community is involved in your story?*

- *What did it take for the heroine in your story to take action?*

If the girls need some prompting to get them going, remind them about the characters and actions in "SuperShelterMakers"—and the big issue that needed to be solved.

Defining Community

Next, transition the girls from their own stories to thinking about real action in a real community—their community. Start by defining community and what it means to the girls.

A community can be any group of individuals who share common interests— real or virtual. A community can be a social group residing in a specific area or one that shares a common heritage. A community can be as simple as a group of organisms—such as plants or animals—living together in a specific region.

Talk with the girls about how natural it is for various communities to overlap. For example, some girls who are Girl Scouts may also be on a soccer team together.

Have them look at Dez's map on page 70 of their books. How many of Dez's communities do they relate to?

Next, ask them to think about mapping their own communities, using page 71 of their book, if they like. Ask:

- *What and where are your real-life communities?*
- *What good things are in your communities?*
- *What do your communities need?*

This is an opportunity to take a look at any news articles the girls have collected—and any ideas that arrived via the Family and Friends Checklists. They might also review pages 74–75 in their book which offer a few "Great Ideas" for Take Action Projects.

The goal is for the girls to gain a clear picture of what's good in the community and what needs improvement. The good reminds the girls to take advantage of what a community offers, and the not-so-good shows where they can improve things. Keep in mind that maps don't have to be traditional. They can take on any imaginative form that the girls dream up.

So by mapping their community, the girls learn to identify community resources and needs. At this phase of the journey, the girls' Girl Scout group is their most basic community. Guide them to see that their own Girl Scout teamwork is the foundation for creating a team with the bigger community. The secure feeling they share in their own group is something that can spiral out into the larger community.

As the girls think over possible Take Action Projects for their community, they'll naturally think about their own beliefs and values. In this way, they can narrow their project choices to an issue they really care about.

Building Consensus: Fist-to-Five

With this activity, the girls come to understand the idea and meaning of *consensus*—that everyone agrees enough to work together.

Now, invite the girls to choose an issue or question they want to decide on as a team—perhaps a trip, an option, or some other "detour" they'd like to experience on their journey.

Then talk about what consensus means. Talk about why it's important to reach a consensus: A team should agree on what it will be doing together so that each team member feels invested in the journey. Each girl should feel that her viewpoint is being heard. When it comes to team decision-making, the consensus-building process ensures that no one feels her view has been ignored.

Talk about what kinds of teams need to reach a consensus. For example:

• a sports team trying to do as well as possible

• a team of architects designing a house

• a team of people starting a new business venture

Next, let the girls know that, as a team, they will use a technique called "Fist-to-Five" to reach a consensus on the topic they've chosen to discuss. Explain that Fist-to-Five is an easy-to-use method that will show the girls how to develop, express, and reach a consensus.[1]

Invite the girls to review the Fist-to-Five hand positions on page 37 of their book and be sure the girls understand them. If anyone holds up fewer than three fingers, they are given the opportunity to state their objections, and the team then addresses their concerns. A team continues the Fist-to-Five process until it achieves consensus (a minimum of three fingers or higher for all team members) or determines it must move on to another issue.

Once the girls have the technique down, they can use it as they move forward exploring the community and talking with its members about possible Take Action Projects. If they've already visited with community members, they may be ready to reach a consensus on their project. If not, they can use Fist-to-Five after they've met with and talked to community members.

---

[1] Fist-to-Five Consensus-Building adapted from Fletcher, A. (2002). *FireStarter Youth Power Curriculum: Participant Guidebook*. Olympia, Wash.: Freechild Project.

Before talking with community members, invite the girls to:

- look over the project possibilities offered on pages 72–75 of their book

- think about the needs and issues they identified in their community maps.

- consider any issues that guest speakers talked to them about.

- offer up any other issues or ideas collected in the team's Take Action Project Possibilities Bank (see page 13 in this guide).

Once the girls are ready with ideas from the community members, invite them to lead their own brainstorming session to narrow their choice to the best possible Take Action Project for them and the community. Invite a girl to write down all the possibilities the team comes up with. Then the girls can get busy with Fist-to-Five and reach a consensus.

Guide the girls to reach a consensus on their Take Action Project. This experience sets the girls on a path to the Power of Community Award. Once they've made their Team Decision, all they need to do is write their Team Hopes—on page 78 of their book.

Moxie up the team

The Real Me?

This activity, on page 24 of the girls' book, is a good complement to thinking about taking action to improve a community. It allows the girls to share who they already are—and their wishes about who they'd like to be. Invite each girl to think of herself as a future leader—a future heroine who's also part of a future Take Action team.

How to Play

Hand out three index cards to each girl.

1. Ask each girl to fill out her cards—one with *True* written on one side and something true about herself on the other (for example, "Nobody knows this, but I have an awesome singing voice—I only use it at home!"), and one with *False* written on it and something not true about her on the back; and one with *Wish* on one side and a wish of the girl on the other.

2. Sit in a circle. Choose the direction the group wants to go.

3. Each girl takes a turn as the speaker. She can say one thing about herself—true, false, or a wish.

4. What does everyone think? The rest of the group has to decide whether what the speaker said was true, false, or a wish. Each girl holds up the card she thinks it is.

5. Now it's the speaker's turn to tell the truth. Who was right? Who was wrong? It's a great way to get to know one another!

6. Afterward, talk about the results. Ask the girls what surprised them.

Keep the mood positive and friendly. You might start by saying:

What if each of us were completely in charge of how to describe ourselves—and no one else? Now's your chance! And the fun part? Only you know the real answer. The rest of us have to guess.

Then the speaker gets to tell what the real answer is, and explain it if she wants.

Say to the girls:

When you wish for something, you often realize something you actually want to change.

REAL "ME" OPTION

Make a set of wish cards—10 wishes, one on each card— and compare and trade them. Suggest that the girls do this on their own later. Or if they need a break, take five and do it now.

Closing Ceremony (optional)

Read this quote to the girls:

"The crowd gives the leader new strength."

—Evenius, Greek writer

Ask the girls to relate the quote to themselves. What does it mean that a crowd gives a leader strength? Why? Ask them to jot down a few ideas. Then talk as a group for a couple of minutes about how the girls interpret the quote. Mention what a joy it is to hear the girls express their enthusiasm over ways to work toward group decision-making.

> "When spider webs unite,
> they can tie up a lion."
>
> —Ethiopian proverb

READY, SET, ACTION!

Everybody Loves PIE!

"STUFF" RESOURCES
Supplies and More

"REALITY" CHECK
(as in, But There're Only, Um, 5 of Us!)

PEOPLE RESOURCES
Cooperation, Communication, and Contacts

Spice Up Your Project

Think About It!

SAMPLE SESSION 5
Ready, Set, Action!

AT A GLANCE

Goal: The girls plan how to take action on their chosen issue and break into project teams to cover every aspect of the project.

- Take Action Project Steps
- Power of Team Award Ceremony
  (optional)
- What Do We Have? Who Do We Have?
- Who Will Do What?
- Time for Reflection

ADVANCE PREP

In this session, as the group plans its Take Action Project, the girls learn key steps for planning and doing a project with the community. Remind the girls that the goal is to make a difference *in the community*. So they want to be as connected as possible with the members of that community. A perfectly executed project isn't as important as the "larger goal": teaming up and working with the community.

This is the time for the girls to visit with community members involved in the issue they've chosen to take action on. They want to be sure they are not simply doing something *for the community*, but doing something *with the community*. Community members might visit with the girls or the girls might go out into the community at various points in the planning process to make sure the project is proceeding in a way that is worthwhile for the community.

Refer to the Take Action Project Checklist on page 19 and guide the girls as needed.

MATERIALS

- Large paper, markers, pens
- Any resources (and/or people) specific to the girls' project

KEEP IT GIRL LED

The Juniors may need to be coached on how to plot out their Take Action Project steps in a way that is both meaningful and workable for the group. But before you take that route, try a full girl-led approach. Use the ideas of "up front" and "behind the scenes" action (see page 76 in the girls' book) to show the variety of ways to take action. The girls can talk in pairs or small groups to share their perspectives about the style they prefer. Suggest that making rough drafts of a plan will help them imagine themselves walking through the Take Action Project steps. Point out that imagining is a major part of getting there.

SCRAPBOOK, ANYONE?

Encourage the girls to take plenty of photos and notes during the entire Take Action Project process, so they can make a scrapbook of all the great work they've accomplished.

Take Action Project Steps

Doing a Take Action Project allows each girl in the group to see herself as an active member of the community—a participant, a community organizer, and a powerful agent of change.

Define *agent* with the girls:

> *Agent:* One who acts or exerts power; one who is authorized to act for, or in place of, another.

Suggest that the girls add any thoughts of their own to this entry in the glossary ("The Power of Words") on page 25 of their books.

Ask the girls to break down their project to its essential steps, as noted on page 79 of their book. They might want to turn these into a "mantra board" for quick and repeated reference. Engage them in assessing every part of the project. Remind them that the project is theirs—it's up to them how they want to do it. Discuss what it means to "own" a project.

Talk about how there is a real progression through the steps, but the girls may not always be moving straight forward. Discuss how they might have to be on two steps at once or even go back a step at times. It helps the girls to see that the *process* of taking action is as important as the results they put into effect.

Power of Team Award Ceremony

By this time, the girls may have completed their experiences for earning their Power of Team Award. Consider stopping for a five-minute ceremony to give out these awards.

It's a team award, so it may make sense for the girls to give the award to one another—in pairs or small groups. And then, back on the Take Action Project express you go!

What Do We Have? Who Do We Have?
Reviewing Resources and Setting Goals

Guide the girls to make their own inventory of all the people, time, and supplies they have or will need for planning and executing their project. Have them detail any community members they need to reach out to and how they will do so (will the girls talk with them by phone or visit them in person, or will they come speak with the girls?).

Then, ask the girls to put their goals in focus:

- *Given the supplies, contacts, and time, are your goals realistic?*

- *Should you adjust them? Scale back?*

Ask the girls if they are confident that they can achieve their goals. "Take the temperature" of the group and see how the girls feel about the project. If they seem unsure, you may want to share an example from your own experience of how to scale back or change something to achieve a goal. Share any experiences you've had when your instincts helped with an outcome. Talk about any doubts they might have. What are some hurdles they may have to overcome? Talk about "expecting the unexpected."

TIME OUT TO JAM

Hold a talking "jam session" to bring out all the ideas, feelings, fears, and energy the girls have regarding bringing the project to the surface.

Share your own feelings about what the girls are doing. Then ask them what they might like to ask you.

If a girl brings up something that bugs her, listen. With a little creative listening, one of the girl's thoughts may become a key component of the Take Action Project.

NO TRAVEL REQUIRED!

If you and the Juniors have limited time or ability to get out and about, simply focus on a Take Action Project that can be done as close to home as possible—perhaps even as a school project during the school day.

Everybody Loves Pie

Drawing a resource pie is a great way to assess resources and is a useful visual aid for dividing into teams.

The girls can use the pie on page 81 in their books or the team can make a big team pie. Use markers, poster board, stars, and photos. Encourage girl-led directions on how to fill in the pie. Explain that many organizations use charts to break down tasks in visual ways that keep them clear and accessible for team members.

Bake It Big!

Max out the pie by making it giant-size. To deepen each girl's grasp, have them divide into teams—adding their names to the different sections as they do so—to assess different parts of the project and then tell the whole group what they think.

Share Your Own Experiences

Whenever possible, share with the girls your experiences of being helped by outside contacts and people. Encourage role-playing to become comfortable with reaching out to others. With a quiet group, ask the girls some questions:

- *What can you learn from those you've reached out to in the community?*

- *What are you curious to ask them when you next meet with them?*

- *Do you feel relaxed talking to them?*

- *How might they, or others, assist you further?*

If some girls are more comfortable than others talking to their contacts, perhaps they are willing to step in and represent the group.

Who Will Do What?
Dividing into Task Teams

Ask the girls to break into task teams so that each small task for the project is covered. (As the girls choose their teams, encourage them to base their choices on their skills and powers—match them to the task and make sure each team has what it needs to succeed.)

Have the girls lead their own breakdown of the project's tasks to ensure that they are keeping their eye on their goals, resources, and logistics. Have the girls show their breakdowns in a visual way that the whole group can see: a big poster, a chart, placards, or a handout that the girls keep, share, and add to their project scrapbooks after the project day.

Every angle of the project should be covered and connected to each girl's sense of her own strengths and skills. Discuss strengths and passions, and how work goes faster when you love what you do. Who's best at what? What needs does each particular challenge fill? Who wants which challenge? The girls should write their tasks in a Take Action Project Checklist like the one on page 19 of this guide.

Time for Reflection

If there's time, elaborate on the power of team by talking about the Ethiopian proverb "When spider webs unite, they can tie up a lion," which is displayed on page 32 of the girls' book. Start a discussion by:

- building on what the girls think this quote means

- talking about the power of working together—and how taking action as a group builds power.

IT'S NEVER TOO EARLY TO THINK AHEAD

As a last activity before the girls delve into their projects, ask them how they want to structure the last step of their Take Action Project: Reflect and Celebrate. Make sure they allow time to reflect on and reward themselves for what they've done at the end, even if it means adding more time to the journey. Share expressions that the girls may relate to, such as: "It's the journey, not the arrival, that matters."

PREPARING FOR TAKE ACTION PROJECT DAYS

On project days, everything should be ready to go. Follow the team's Take Action Project Checklist and draw on the support and participation of parents, older Girl Scouts, and any other resources you want to bring into the effort. Take pictures, do interviews, or have the girls record one another's thoughts and their own.

"I learned that I can accomplish a large task one step at a time."

—Amy Poe, community organizer

Time for the Take Action Project

AT A GLANCE

Goal: The girls carry out their Take Action Project and then reflect on and celebrate the change they accomplished.

- The Project Checklist
- Project Day Inspiration
- After the Take Action Project: Reflecting on the Journey
- Celebrating
- Circling Back to Reflect One More Time
- A Story in Your Group's Honor
- Project Day Scrapbook
- Award Ceremony

STRENGTH IN NUMBERS

Depending on the project and where it takes place, you may need additional adult assistance. Present these "reinforcements" to the girls as "strength in numbers," not as additional authority figures. Encourage the girls to brainstorm about how parents, siblings, older Girl Scouts, and others can help them on project days. Adult-youth teamwork is essential to any real community effort, so encourage adults to join the girls on the teams— it's a good learning opportunity for all.

MAKING MEMORIES

Encourage the girls to keep a record of their experiences by taking photos and making notes for their project scrapbooks. If possible, have someone videotape or photograph parts of the event. Some girls may want to be part-time "record-keepers" or "memory makers" who take pictures, do interviews, and report on the project days.

Keep Community Front and Center

In these sessions, the group executes its Take Action Project. Encourage the girls to experience this project as something creative and something to enjoy. Keep the community element in the forefront. Remind them that going into the community to bring about change is a *remarkable* thing to do. It's also a chance to learn from new people.

The Take Action Project won't have to end when the girls' project is completed. In some cases, it will have just begun.

Along the way, as a framework and a "reality check," remind the girls that projects can take on a life of their own. (See **"After the Take Action Project: Reflection and Celebration"** on page 82 of this book for more perspective-enhancing tips on the Take Action Project.)

The ideas offered for reflecting, celebrating, and keeping the journey's memories alive are simply suggestions. The project itself may leave little time for more than one or two of these activities. What's important is that the project be meaningful for the girls and that they have time to reflect on and celebrate what they've done. You and the girls may even take time for a celebration just right for agents of change.

The Project Checklist

Have the girls keep their Take Action Project Checklists handy—they'll help keep things as organized as possible as project days approach.

Project Day Inspiration

Pick and choose from the list of activities on the next page, depending on the project your group is doing. As always, the activities are meant to be adapted to the girls' needs. Whenever possible, encourage the girls to lead them.

Great Inspirations Station

This activity adds layers to the action project and encourages creativity, appeals to the audience and community involved in the project, and draws attention to the project, too!

Encourage some upbeat brainstorming to create funny and slightly irreverent slogans. Use the examples to jog creativity. Girls who are into art can make the big board, girls who are good with music can record thematically related songs, and girls who like to do research can come up with inspirational leaders of the past.

You Rock! Poster

A poster is a great way to thank the members of the community for their participation in the project. Talk with the girls about how good it feels to be acknowledged and thanked as an individual. What would be a good way to include everyone and each individual at the same time?

Scrapbook Worth Keeping

Instead of a poster, make the thank you part of the Project Day Scrapbook (see page 85), and give it to all the members of the community who participated.

And the Winner Is

Celebrate the accomplishments of the community involved in the project (which keeps the focus on what's really important—community). Discuss what kind of tasks the community is doing as part of the project. The girls might create award certificates and prizes, perhaps using items related to the project. Hold a ceremony at the end of the project to present them.

Continue the Community Spirit

How about a girl-led award ceremony to deepen and continue the group's relationship with the community involved in the project? Discuss what the girls want to recognize and celebrate with the community. It's up to the girls. Talk about the power of encouragement and acknowledgment.

Community Guests

Invite community members to the girls' final awards ceremony and hold a special awards segment for them, too.

TAKE FIVE AND HUDDLE

Just as in sports, each team may need a moment to regroup. So have the girls let you know when they need to huddle. Be sure to take time to keep everybody on track during the project.

If the girls don't ask for a Take Five, call one when you feel the time is right. Relate it to the girls' sense of themselves as community organizers: Explain that they may need this chance to take a moment to make sure they're all on task with the Take Action Project.

After the Take Action Project: Reflecting on the Journey

All along, you've encouraged the girls to reflect on activities, actions, and their ideas. Now they'll reflect on and celebrate their accomplishments.

Go over the most important lessons of the Take Action Project with the group:

REFLECT (BUT DON'T REDO)

Guide the girls through the "debriefing" process. They can decide their own process here. Redirect it only if they're trying to spin it into "if only we could have done it differently." Explain that this is about emphasizing the positive, and that they all deserve a round of applause. Then lead them in that rousing round of applause!

- Encourage the girls to feel great about becoming community organizers. Remind them that you have to get into the community and be part of it to make a difference. Discuss what that means. Even if they're making phone calls or writing letters to send around the world, they're making an effort to make a difference.

- Encourage the girls to feel great about their project—however small it may seem, it is big for the girls. Remind them that a project may seem like a drop in the bucket, but it's an enormous drop! Discuss what it means to spread the effect. When you involve different people, the effects are like a tree growing into a dozen, then a hundred, then a million, branches. Sometimes, all it takes to get a community going is one action.

- Make sure the girls understand the value of their actions throughout this journey. The Take Action Project is the culmination of a journey of self-discovery and team-building, all the while using leadership skills.

- Discuss how the girls feel now compared to when they started the journey: Have they gained confidence?

- Discuss the element of chance and process—the value of enjoying the journey as it unfolds as well as the final destination.

- Emphasize the importance of the community; the relationships with people the girls have met can be continued and deepened. Just because the Take Action Project days are over doesn't mean the project can't continue in a long-term way.

Celebrating

Opposite and in the girls' book are a variety of activities to help the girls celebrate everything they accomplished by creating, planning, and completing a Take Action Project. Invite the girls to decide which ones they'd like to do. Plan out a future meeting to do up the celebration and the presentation of the journey's culminating award. Don't let the girls forget about displaying their collages, *her*stories, and power stories.

"Plan Big"

Display the text on page 85 of the girls' book that begins, "Plan big because you made the journey from . . ." Write it on the blackboard or a sheet of poster board for the girls to anchor to as they move through the celebration. Have the girls lead you through the text as you write it.

Pull Out the Positive: A "Draw Straws" Activity

This activity celebrates the girls' accomplishments and breaks down their experiences topically. Once the straws are created, the girls gather together and, one by one, choose a straw and tell a story about an experience from their Take Action Project that "captures" what's on their straw.

You'll Need:

1 container, such as a can, with 20 labeled straws in it. Using stickers or masking tape or something fancier, label the straws with topics that relate to the project.

Sample labels for straws (make duplicate labels as needed):

- Community
- Teamwork among us
- Teamwork with outside people
- Speed at which we worked
- Good moment
- Really amazing moment

- Aha moment
- Scary moment
- Moxie moment
- Organizer extraordinaire moment
- Oops moment
- How we communicated
- Our effectiveness
- Our power to make a difference
- Timing and schedule
- Materials
- Transportation

Clap Your Hands and Say Thanks

This is a chance to "testify" and thank those who mattered to each girl during the Take Action Project. And the girls should (loudly!) thank one another, too.

Community Proclamation

This is a way to put the group's commitment to the project and the community in writing—and pass it on, if the girls want, for posterity and the next group.

Ask the girls to write a proclamation about their continuing commitment to the community that their project has focused on. Keep up the good work with a serious promise! Frame it and present it to the organizers you worked with.

Change It Up for the Future

The girls may choose to attach an amendment to their proclamation that describes what they'd like to change about the project in the future. Possibilities: more breaks for stretching, more advance work to get the media interested, more cookies at the meetings, custom T-shirts that say COMMUNITY ORGANIZER EXTRAORDINAIRE.

Another Rope Ceremony

If the girls have carried forward the rope ceremony they began in Session 1, now's the time for a final, powerful rope ceremony. The girls will likely want to revisit that first "rope poster," too, to see how much they've accomplished on the journey.

Circling Back to Reflect One More Time

Check back with **"What Makes Me *Me*? Or, I'm Being Framed!"** activity from Session 1. Ask the girls to compare what they said then to the sense of themselves that they have now. It's amazing how much a person can grow in just weeks!

Ask:

How were you on target?

Has the way you see yourself changed at all? If so, how?

A Story In Your Group's Honor

Encourage the girls to use the end pages of their book to make a comic-book-style story of their project—or their whole journey. Say something like: *Now that you've finished your project, why not commemorate it with a fantastically drawn and totally fun comic about it? You can take the comic-book idea and redo it in your group's honor. You've even got space set aside for it in the back of your book!*

Their story might be "SuperLetterWriters," "SuperFoodDrivers," "SuperGardenCreators—Super whatever their project was about.

Project Day Scrapbook

Making a scrapbook will give the Take Action Project and the journey even more meaning and resonance in the years to come. Let the girls lead the way with this one.

Award Ceremony

Do it big or do it small—just be sure to do it in the way the girls have chosen and planned.

Now, Take Some Time for Yourself

When the girls' reflection and celebration is over, take time to do your own celebrating and reflecting. You've guided a group of Girl Scout Juniors on an amazing journey to becoming agents of change. That's no small accomplishment. Look back at the reflection exercise you tried at the beginning of the journey (see page 36–39). How have your answers changed?

Have you gained any new heroines? Are any of them Girl Scout Juniors?

_____

_____

_____

Did the Power of Team experienced by the girls give you a new perspective on the power of teamwork?

_____

_____

_____

When the girls combined the Power of Team and Power of Community, were you inspired by their actions? What's the next thing _you_ will do to be an agent of change?

_____

_____

_____

_____